The
Biting Book

The Biting Book

by
Judi Friedman

illustrated by
Kees de Kiefte

Prentice-Hall, Inc., Englewood Cliffs, N.J.

Prentice-Hall International, Inc., London
Prentice-Hall of Australia, Pty. Ltd., North Sydney
Prentice-Hall of Canada, Ltd., Toronto
Prentice-Hall of India Private Ltd., New Delhi
Prentice-Hall of Japan, Inc., Tokyo

JAN '77 5.95

Library of Congress Cataloging in Publication Data

Friedman, Judith Cron.
  The biting book.

  SUMMARY: An introduction to the ways animals use their teeth for eating, playing, and protection.
  1. Animals, Habits and behavior of—Juvenile literature. 2. Teeth—Juvenile literature. [1. Animals—Habits and behavior. 2. Teeth]
I. De Kiefte, Kees. II. Title.
QL751.5.F7   596′.05′3   75-11537
ISBN 0-13-077263-1

1-4

To Kim, Dana, Seth, and Lou

BIRNEY

The little brown bat sweeps bugs into her mouth
with her wings as she flies. Then she uses her teeth
to kill the insects.

Many animals eat meat just as people do. Since animals do not have hands that can hold guns or knives, they must use their teeth and their paws for catching their food.

The gray fox, a good mother, spends many hours teaching her pups how to catch mice.

Over and over the pups watch her catch a mouse in her teeth and then shake it until it is dead.

The little red squirrel
uses his teeth
like a nutcracker.

The striped chipmunk also uses his teeth to peel
away the outside husk of an acorn.

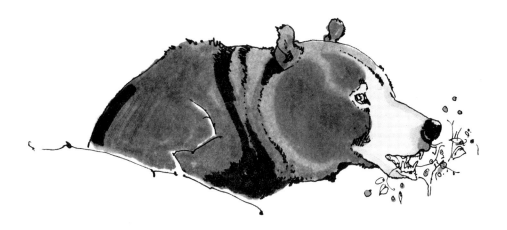

Because animals do not have hands to hold silverware, they use their teeth as people use tools like knives and forks.

Although the black bear likes blueberries, he cannot use a spoon. He pulls the berries from the branches with his teeth and gets a lot of leaves and twigs in his mouth at the same time.

The white-tailed deer cuts the grass with his teeth.

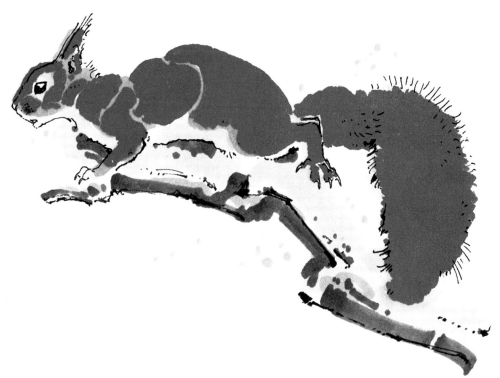

The little gray squirrel has a piece missing from his ear. He was eating too near another larger squirrel.

Animals use their teeth for biting when they like each other. They cannot kiss, so a gentle bite on the neck or nose may mean "I love you."

The male wolf nips the ears, face and the back of his friend. He wags his tail. Together they run off into the woods.

The stallion faces the mare. Then he moves closer and bites the side of her neck.

She likes him, so she does not mind.

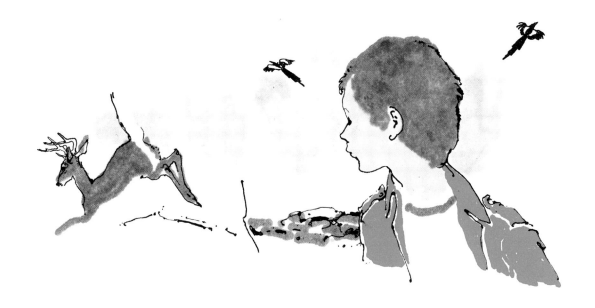

Animals do not usually use their teeth for biting people.

Wild animals almost always try to hide from you. If you try to run after them, animals go away. That is why it is so hard to see most animals. They are afraid of you.

You seem big. You are noisy. You smell funny to them.

The black bear
hears very well.
Although she is very big,
she runs quickly
into the woods when
she hears your voice.

The fox sneaks quietly
behind a brush pile.

The porcupine
will waddle to a tree
and climb it.

The deer will jump away. (You may be lucky enough to see her white tail.)

The bat will not fly into you. Bats make little noises that bounce off anything that is near. These noises keep them from bumping into things.

Some animals may bite by mistake.

The horse that you are feeding may bite your hand as he eats. If you hold your hand flat, he cannot make that mistake!

A dog that is playing roughly may tear your sweater because he is excited. He forgets how strong he is!

A raccoon on the road that has been hurt by a car may bite the person who is trying to help him.

The raccoon thinks the person looks strange. He smells strange to the raccoon, too. And the person may hurt the raccoon as he lifts him up.

The black snake may bite the person who tries to pick her up.

Because she is hurt and frightened, she will try to bite anyone who steps on her.

You would probably try to bite or hit a giant if he or she stepped on you or tried to pick you up!

There are a few times when an animal will bite because it is sick.

A wild animal with a sickness called "rabies" will not act as it usually does; it will act strange.

It may seem friendly. You may see it in the middle of the day although it is an animal that usually moves around at night.

The fox who has rabies may not run away.

He may even come toward you, but if you do not go near him, he cannot bite you.

Sometimes wild animals will bite if they are in cages.

They do not like to be in cages any more than you would like being locked in a room.

The caged coyote is mean and feels angry.

Sometimes animals bite because they are confused and do not understand. Although some animals are used to people, they are still wild.

Sometimes they feel friendly. They know that people feed them.

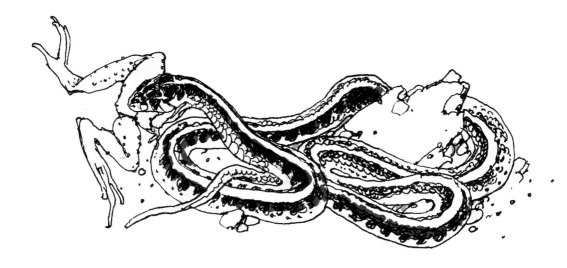

The garter snake eats his food alive.

Because the food that he catches is often larger than he is, it takes him a long time to swallow his dinner. So he uses his teeth to hold his food in his mouth.

A dog has no hands to take away the flea that is biting him so he uses his teeth to bite the tiny flea.

Most animals have teeth. They use their teeth in many different ways.

Sometimes animals use their teeth in the same way that people use their hands.

One of the red fox's babies has crawled too far away from his mother.

Gently, she lifts him up with her teeth and carries him to the safety of her den.

Sometimes animals use their teeth for fighting each other.

Two male animals may fight because they are both interested in the same female.

On a moonlit night two large male raccoons bite each other and make growling noises. The female watches. When the fight is over, she will choose whom she likes best!

Sometimes one animal may hunt too near another animal. Then the animals may bite each other.

Sometimes one of the animals will run away. Then the fight is over.

Animals do not fight people unless they are teased.

It is not a good idea to feed animals that live in one of our national parks. If you give her a cookie on a day when she is unhappy, she may bite your arm too.

Animals that have babies may bite you. They want to keep their babies safe and they are afraid that you will hurt their babies. The animals will not run away and leave their children.

A bear will become angry if you are too near her cubs.

Even your cat may worry if you touch her kittens.
Think how your mother would act if a huge hand
came out of nowhere and picked you up.

But most animals will not bite you. They just want to be left alone.

They want to take care of their babies, be warm and have enough to eat and drink—just like you and your family.

There is only one animal that will not run away from you when you are in the woods.

She will not hide in a den or under a rock. She will not climb a tree. Although she is very small and does not have any teeth, she will come near you and try to "bite" you.

Do you know what she is?

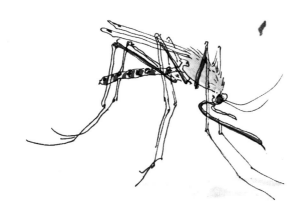

She is a mosquito.